STEP·BY·STEP

GOLF

Eddie Birchenough and Alistair Tait

GALLERY BOOKS

An Imprint of W.H. Smith Publishers Inc.

112 Madison Avenue
New York City 10016

© **The Automobile Association, 1990**
Fanum House,
Basing View,
Basingstoke RG21 2EA
United Kingdom

ISBN: 0-8317-8050-9

This edition published in 1991 by Gallery Books, an imprint of W.H. Smith Publishers, Inc., 112 Madison Avenue, New York, New York 10016

Gallery Books are available for bulk purchase for sales promotions and premium use. For details write or telephone the Manager of Special Sales, W.H. Smith Publishers, Inc., 112 Madison Avenue, New York, New York 10016. (212) 532-6600

The contents of this book are believed correct at the time of printing. Nevertheless, the Publishers cannot accept any responsibility for any errors or omissions in the details given.

CREDITS

Authors: Eddie Birchenough and Alistair Tait
Photography: Matthew Harris
Illustrations: Oxford Illustrators Ltd.

Typesetting by Microset Graphics Ltd., Basingstoke, United Kingdom
Color separation by Fotographics Ltd., London and Hong Kong
Printed and bound by L.E.G.O. SpA, Italy

Cover and title page: Nick Faldo at the 1989 Masters (Matthew Harris)

CONTENTS

FOREWORD

The world is full of people who are willing to give advice. Whether or not they are qualified to give advice, though, is the important question you must ask yourself. Golf is no exception to this rule.

Every person who has ever lifted a club is, it seems, an expert — always willing to give you guidance and set you on the correct path to better golf. More often than not, such advice usually ends up sending you into abject misery, pushing scores ever higher and complicating the golf swing so that no matter how athletic you may be, you find it impossible even to make contact with the ball, let alone build a swing that will make this frustrating game easy.

As a young man I was given endless advice on the correct way to swing a golf club. I found that most of it was incorrect. Eventually I stopped listening to amateurs and started watching the professionals, talking to them, taking notes as I did so, revising my theory constantly, and replacing what I had once seen as sound practice with the essential mechanics of the swing.

Even after 25 years of watching and working with some of the best players in the world, I am still learning. Great golfers seem to swing the club so simply that you wonder why you have so much trouble getting the ball airborne, let alone on to the green. These players have stripped the game of all its complications, concentrating on simply swinging the clubhead. Years of practice have shown them that by concentrating on fundamentals, they can play golf at the highest level.

You might not be able to play to the same standard as the professionals, but you *can* build a swing that will enable you to play golf well for life, provided that you learn and live by the fundamentals.

This book doesn't give you complicated theories that will put your body into contortions the minute you pick up a club. What it does give you is a thorough grounding in golf's essentials, so that no matter what club you have in your hand — from a driver to a putter — you will know what to do to play the game to the best of your ability.

The text in this book aims to keep instruction as simple as possible, and places emphasis on the photographs and illustrations. STAR TIPS from the best players in professional golf are also included so that you can apply their techniques to your own game. All the techniques in this book have been given difficulty ratings. These are shown by one, two or three golfers at the top of each spread. One golfer shows a technique that is relatively simple to master, while three indicate a skill that is more difficult to acquire.

Everything that I have learned about the essentials of the game in nearly 25 years of professional golf is included in this book. Learn the techniques explained here, and you will enjoy golf for the rest of your life.

Eddie Birchenough

Eddie Birchenough

An aerial view of Royal Lytham and St. Anne's — site of numerous British Open Championships. Eddie Birchenough is head professional here.
INSET: Seve Ballesteros holds aloft the British Open trophy, which he won at Royal Lytham in 1988.

LEARN THE FUNDAMENTALS

No one is quite sure how the game of golf started. Some say it began as a form of ice hockey on frozen ponds in Holland. Others say its origins lie on the links land, along the coast of Scotland's kingdom of Fife, where shepherds are said to have whiled away their days by improvising shots with crooks and small stones. It doesn't really matter.

What does matter is that ever since the first person hit a small round object with a wooden club and watched it soar off into the distance, *Homo sapiens* has been fascinated with golf.

The game has gone through many stages since that first "golfer" felt the exhilaration of a well-struck shot. In the early days, budding Ballesteroses and Nicklauses would fill a leather pouch with feathers — hence the "feathery" — pound it roughly into a spherical shape, and attempt to hit this imperfect object straight. Later still, Malaysian gum, or *gutta percha*, was discovered. Using hot water, this was rolled into a sphere and allowed to harden, creating a perfectly round golf ball for the first time. The modern ball was invented by Coburn Haskell, who developed a soft-cored, elastic-wound ball, complete with dimples.

Golfers used crude instruments made with hickory shafts in those early days. Today, people the world over play with all the advantages of modern technology. Hickory shafts have been replaced with graphite, titanium and beryllium, not to mention steel. The novice golfer no longer has to take only what is available in the professional's shop. Nowadays golfers can get equipment built specifically to their individual requirements.

The modernization of equipment has changed the basic way in which people swing the golf club. In the days prior to steel shafts, players had to have strong hands and forearms to accommodate the torque created by hickory shafts. That was why the early swing included a lot of hand action.

New technology has made it possible to play the game without the forearms of an axeman. Good golfers use the whole body in the swing, pulling the club through with the body to propel it toward the target.

Anyone who watches great players does so with awe. They seem to play a game that is totally alien to the majority of golfers throughout the world. However, although not everyone will go on to win the greatest championships in professional golf, anyone who wants to learn the game and play to a reasonable standard can do so by applying the techniques of the professionals to his own game.

Someone once said that golf was never meant to be fair. Neither was it meant to be a painful experience. There are only a few fundamentals that need to be mastered to play golf well, and this book teaches you about them. Once you have mastered the fundamentals, you will find that golf will be fair to you.

José Maria Olazabal of Spain demonstrates the perfect position at impact, which results from strict adherence to the basic fundamentals.

KNOW YOUR EQUIPMENT

THE GRIP

The most vital element of a golf club, and the one that is most ignored, is the grip. It is your only connection with the clubhead, and any chance of playing good golf will be destroyed if the club is fitted with an improper grip.

To test whether or not the grips on your clubs are the correct size, simply take the club in your left hand and check the relationship between the fingers and the palm of the hand. The fingers should just touch the palm of the hand.

Seve Ballesteros and Sandy Lyle compare the differences in their drivers. Notice how one grip is made of leather, while the other is made of rubber.

Grips nowadays are made of leather (left), rubber (middle), or cord (right). Rubber is the most popular.

1 Steel (bottom), graphite (middle), and boron (top) are just a few of the materials used for making clubshafts.

2 Metal woods (left) are taking over from traditional woods (right) because better weight distribution is more forgiving on off-center hits.

3 Forged clubheads (bottom) and investment cast clubheads (top) differ in terms of weight distribution. In investment cast heads, the weight is distributed around the edges, allowing the player to get the ball airborne more easily.

ADVICE

The best person to consult when purchasing or replacing a set of clubs is a professional. Only he will be able to properly judge whether the clubs you want are suited to your game and physique or not.

THE SHAFT

Shafts nowadays come in many materials, and getting a shaft that suits your game is vitally important. Too stiff a shaft will mean that you won't be able to square the clubface at impact, leading to shots which end up straying to the right. Too flexible a shaft will make the clubface tend to close at address and result in shots flying to the left.

THE CLUBHEAD

Irons are made nowadays with two types of heads: forged and investment cast steel. Forged clubs tend to have weight concentrated in the back of the club, and the ball tends to fly low. These clubs are favored by professionals because of their softer feel.

Weight is generally placed in the edges of the club in investment cast clubs. Such clubs produce a shot which flies high. These clubs are favored by average golfers, as they allow them to get the ball airborne easily. The design produces a larger hitting area on the clubface, so that a ball that is struck off-center will still fly some distance. This theory has also been applied to metal woods; off-center hits on a metal wood are more forgiving than on traditional woods.

THE IMPORTANCE OF LIE

The lie of the club is the angle between the clubhead and the shaft when the player is in the correct address position. It is important that the sole of the club lie flat on the turf when the player addresses the ball.

THE BASIC GRIP

To play golf to any degree of excellence you must first have a sound grip. This is something most golfers ignore. Yet once you have the grip right, many problems can be solved.

The grip needs to be effective to do four basic tasks:

- deliver the clubface squarely to the back of the ball,
- allow the wrists to hinge correctly during the swing,
- keep the hands ahead of the ball and firmly on the grip at the point of impact,
- transmit power through to the ball.

Besides these four important tasks, the grip allows you to feel the weight of the club as it passes through its arc.

It is essential to get this first fundamental correct, as the only contact you have with the ball is through the grip to the clubhead. Your hands need to control the clubhead at all times during the swing if you are to strike the ball squarely and transmit the body's power through the hands into the back of the ball.

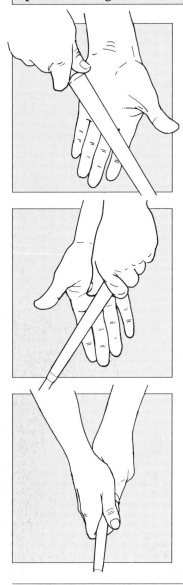

THE LEFT HAND
Place the grip of the club diagonally across the palm of your left hand, just above the fingers. It should sit just above the little finger under the butt pad of the hand and run down to the forefinger of the left hand. Then simply close the hand around the grip. The left thumb should sit to the right of the grip, and the V created by the thumb and forefinger should point toward the right shoulder. The clubshaft and left arm should form a straight line.

THE RIGHT HAND
The club is held by the middle two fingers of the right hand. You can wrap the right little finger over the left forefinger in the basic Vardon grip; interlock the two fingers in an interlocking grip; or place the hands close together in the baseball grip. Then wrap your right palm over your left thumb, so that the right thumb sits to the left of the shaft; the V formed by the thumb and forefinger points to the right shoulder.

THE COMPLETE GRIP
When you look down at the complete grip, you should see two-and-a-half or three knuckles on the back of the left hand. It is essential that the hands work as one unit throughout the swing. Your primary purpose is to control the clubface. A good grip allows you to do this.

THE VARDON GRIP
A close-up of Spanish sensation José Maria Olazabal's Vardon grip. The overlapping of the little finger of the right hand over the index finger of the left welds the hands together into one unit.

STAR TIP
Jack Nicklaus believes in keeping the grip as natural as possible by setting the hands parallel to each other. In this way the hands work together, not against each other.

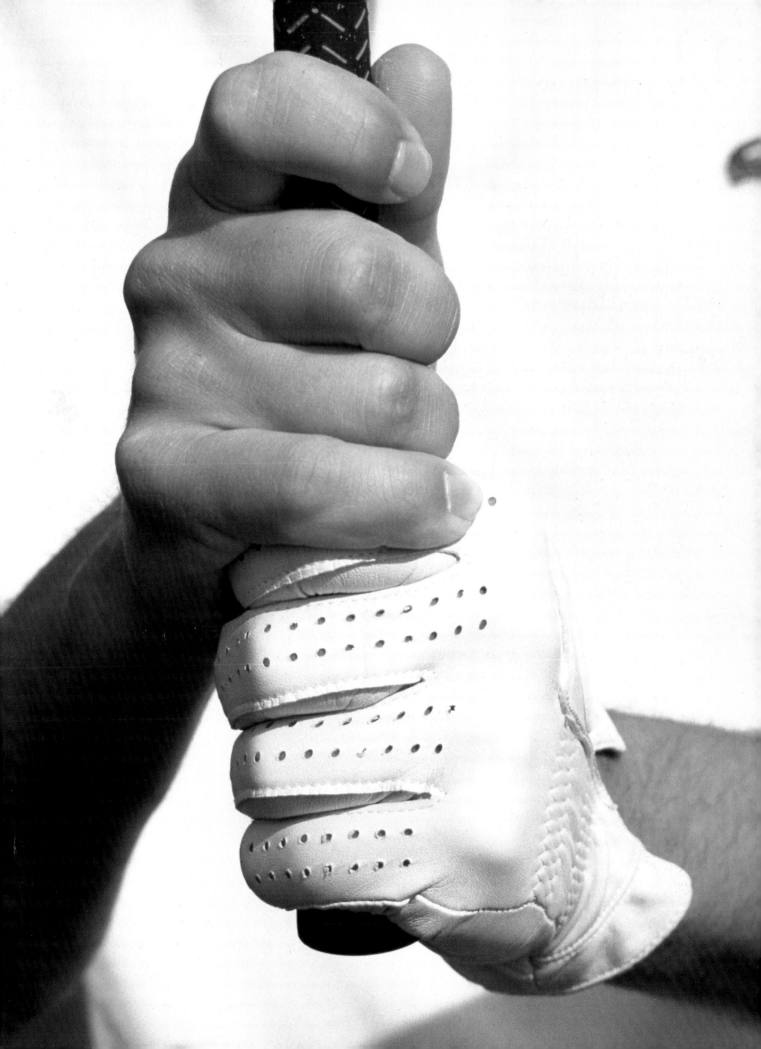

WEAK, STRONG AND NEUTRAL GRIPS

As we have already seen, the relationship between the hands on the grip and the clubhead determines whether or not the clubface is squared at impact. There are only three positions the clubface can be in at impact: open, closed or square.

A weak grip is one in which the hands sit very much to the left of the shaft. Golfers who tend to point their left thumbs straight down the shaft play with a weak grip. In such a grip the Vs of both hands point straight up toward or to the left of the chin, and the hands will be behind the ball at address.

Because the hands will naturally try to return to a neutral position at impact, with a weak grip the player will find it harder to square the clubface at impact. The face of the club will be open, and the ball will fly to the right. Usually this grip leads to the dreaded slice.

A strong grip is the reverse of the weak grip, with the hands turned too far to the right on the handle. Usually, nearly four knuckles are seen on the left hand, and the Vs of the hands point away from the body rather than toward the right shoulder. As with the weak grip, the hands will try to return to a neutral position at impact, and a strong grip will close the clubface, resulting in shots which move left of the target.

In the correct grip, the back of the left hand and the palm of the right hand work in unison, both facing the target. The Vs point toward your right shoulder, and you should be able to see two-and-a-half to three knuckles of the left hand. With this grip, you do not have to manipulate the hands unnaturally during the swing to square the clubface. A neutral grip allows the hands to transmit the power created by the body into the back of the ball. You can concentrate on letting the big muscles of the body create energy during the swing. This grip will return the hands to a neutral position at impact with a square clubface, and shots will fly straight toward the target.

The proper grip will place the hands ahead of the clubface correctly. This is vital, as it allows the club to swing into the ball from slightly inside the target line with the clubhead accelerating. This is necessary to produce a solid strike.

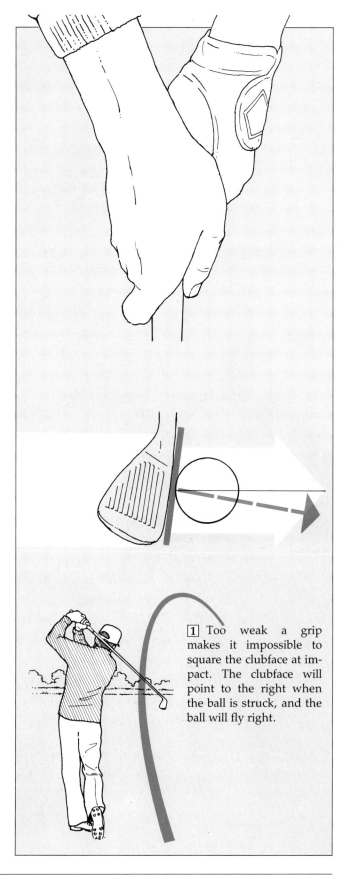

1 Too weak a grip makes it impossible to square the clubface at impact. The clubface will point to the right when the ball is struck, and the ball will fly right.

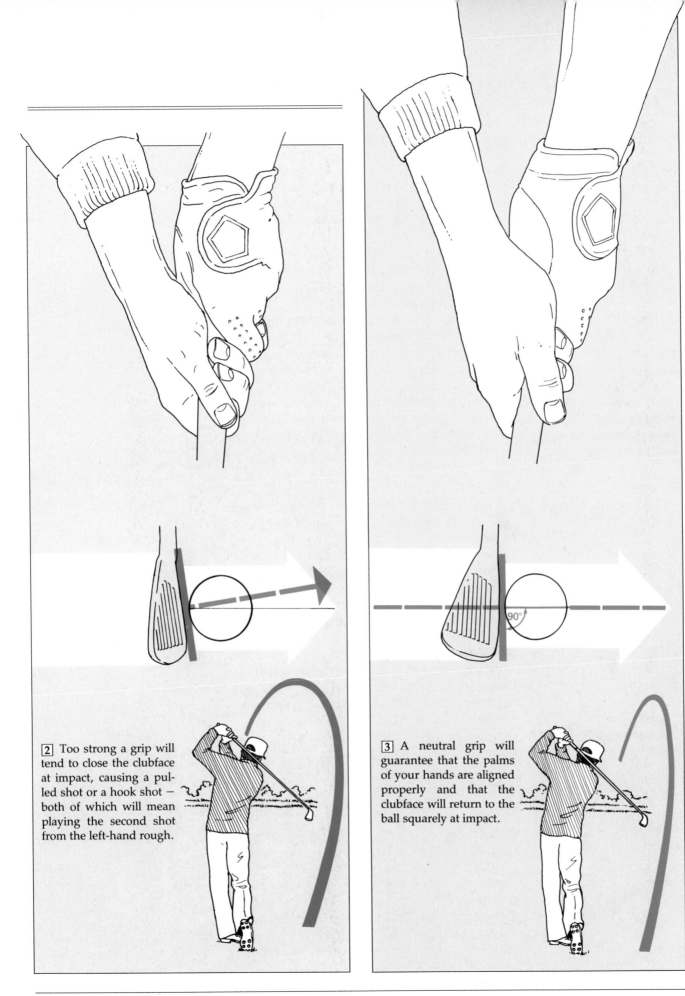

2 Too strong a grip will tend to close the clubface at impact, causing a pulled shot or a hook shot — both of which will mean playing the second shot from the left-hand rough.

3 A neutral grip will guarantee that the palms of your hands are aligned properly and that the clubface will return to the ball squarely at impact.

90°

STANCE AND POSTURE

Adopting the proper stance and posture will ensure that the club travels on the correct arc. In order to swing on the correct line toward the target, you must check that your body is aligned parallel to the target line (the line running from the ball to the flag or target). The relationship between your body, particularly the shoulders, and the target line governs the path along which the clubhead swings. The club has to approach the ball directly along the target line if the ball is to be propelled straight at the target.

It is important, then, to keep your feet, knees, hips and shoulders parallel to the target line. If the body is aligned to the left of the target, the club will approach the ball from outside the target line, or out-to-in. Conversely, the club will approach the ball from inside the target line, or in-to-out, if the body is aimed to the right of the target.

Posture is equally important if you are to return the clubhead on the correct angle at impact. You should not approach the ball at too steep an angle, or on too flat an angle. Your posture governs the angle of approach and the plane of your swing.

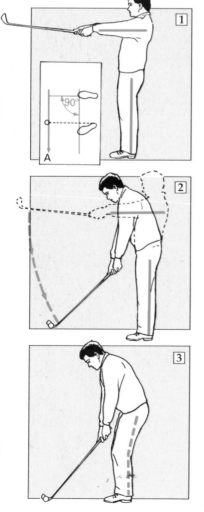

STEP 1
Align your body parallel to the target line (A) and distribute the weight evenly between your two feet. Make sure your body weight is on the balls of your feet, and not on the toes or the heels. This will allow you to maintain your balance throughout the swing.

Place the right foot at a right angle to the target, and point your left foot out toward the target slightly. By placing the feet in this manner you will ensure the proper hip turn on the backswing, and allow the hips to clear to the left as you swing through the ball.

Now hold the club straight out in front of you so that it is horizontal to the ground. Keep the left arm and clubshaft in a straight line.

STEP 2
Next, keep the legs straight and bend from the waist until the clubhead touches the ground.

STEP 3
Now allow your knees to flex slightly. You will be in the correct position to swing the club, having adopted the proper plane for your physique.

SQUARE POSITION
Curtis Strange is in a perfectly square position at address. His feet, knees, hips and shoulders are square to the target line. Notice, too, how his knees are slightly flexed and his arms hang down naturally to give him lots of room to swing the club.

STANCE, POSTURE AND ALIGNMENT

1 In an open stance, the body points to the left of the target, usually resulting in an out-to-in swing path — with the clubhead cutting across the ball. This setup usually results in a pulled shot left of the target, or a slice to the right.

2 The body points right of the target in a closed stance, and the clubhead will approach from inside the target

line. The ball will hook to the left if the clubface is square to the target, or fly straight right if the clubface is open.

3 Only the square stance guarantees that the club-head approaches the ball along the target line.

4 The stance is fairly narrow for the short iron, and the ball is played back in the stance, nearer the center.

5 The stance for the middle iron is a little wider than for the short iron. Notice how the hands are still ahead of the ball at address.

6 For the long iron the feet are nearly a shoulder-width apart, and the hands are not quite as far ahead of the ball as they were for the short and middle irons.

7 Because it is the longest club in the bag, the driver requires the feet to be shoulder-width apart. The hands should also be placed about level with the ball.

8 It will help you aim the clubface if you can find a marker – such as a leaf – directly in line with the clubhead and the target.

9 American Steve Pate takes a good look at the target, standing directly behind the ball. By doing this, he can better position his body at address.

THE BACKSWING

The backswing is important because it creates momentum in the swing, and because it sets the body and club in a position to swing through the ball to the target.

During the backswing, the feet remain firmly on the ground. This means that it is vital to turn and coil your body tightly in order to give power to the swing. You must therefore try to build as much tension between your hips and shoulders as possible. To do this it is important that the hips resist the shoulder turn.

The backswing is initiated by the left arm and shoulder pushing the club away from the target. As the shoulders begin to turn, the club will move inside the target line, into the proper path. You should refrain from turning your hips until they are pulled around by the shoulders. At this point, the toe of the club should be pointing straight up.

At the top of the swing, the weight of the body should be completely transferred onto the right leg, and the club should be horizontal and pointing at the target. This is the perfect position from which to start the downswing.

STEP 1

The backswing is started by the left hand and arm pushing the club back from the ball. The shoulders follow soon after, and the hips do not turn until the shoulders begin to pull them. This should take place when the club is horizontal to the ground.

STEP 2

At hip height (A), the toe of the club should be pointing straight up and the hips should be resisting the turn. It is at this stage in the swing that the wrists begin to hinge. They should do so naturally, due to the weight of the clubhead.

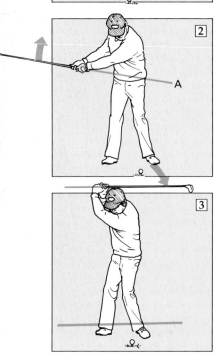

STEP 3

At the top of the swing the club should be horizontal to the ground and the weight should be on the right leg. The shoulders will be at 90 degrees to the target (with the back facing the target), while the hips will only have turned half that distance. When the hips turn back to the left to initiate the downswing, the power created by the coil can be released naturally into the back of the ball. It is a common misconception that the head should remain steady in the backswing. Very few players can actually do this. Concentrate instead on the back of the ball during the backswing.

PERFECT POSITION
Nick Faldo (England) is in the perfect position at the top of the backswing. Notice how the back is facing the target and the hips have resisted the shoulder turn. He is now in the perfect position to pull the club down into the ball. INSET: Ian Woosnam in action.

STAR TIP

Ian Woosnam (Wales) hits the ball a long way for a small man. One of his secrets lies in the easy manner with which he swings the club. Woosnam's only purpose in the backswing is to get the club into the proper position at the top of the swing to allow him to strike the ball. You should make that your purpose, too.

THE DOWNSWING

The split second when the backswing ends and the downswing begins is the moment of truth in every golf swing. You may have a perfect grip, good stance and posture, excellent alignment, and a sound backswing, but the beginning of the downswing will determine whether or not the shot will be a good one.

At the top of a good backswing, a power source has been created, and the correct arc for the clubhead has been established. It is important that the club return to the ball correctly in order for the power created to be unleashed into the back of the ball.

During the backswing, the pull of the shoulders and upper body is resisted by the lower half of the body, the legs and the hips.

All you have to do to initiate the downswing is release the lower body, and then pull down and through with the left arm and side into the back of the ball. In this way the swing works as a chain reaction, with every action setting up another reaction. The unwinding of the hips releases the shoulders; the shoulders pull the arms down and through; and then the hands transmit power into the shot in turn.

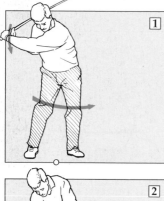

STEP 1

The beginning of the downswing is initiated by turning the left hip and side back toward the target. This, in turn, sets up a chain reaction, whereby the power created by the resistance of the hips and shoulders is transferred into the back of the ball. As the hips turn back to the target, the shoulders are pulled around. The left arm pulls the club down toward the ball in turn, and the wrists uncock as the club approaches the ball.

STEP 2

At impact, the head is behind the ball, the right knee is kicking in toward the target, and the weight is mostly on the left foot. The hands are ahead of the clubface at this point.

STEP 3

Just after impact, the hands have released and the head is beginning to face the target. The weight is now on the left foot and the hips have cleared fully to the left. Resist the tendency to lift the head to see the ball fly towards the target. Stay focused on the ball for as long as possible and let the turning of your shoulders bring your head around to the target.

AFTER IMPACT
Just after impact, Nick Faldo's right hand has turned over his left, indicating that he has released the hands through impact. The flying turf also shows that Faldo has hit down and through the ball.

THE COMPLETE SWING SEQUENCE

1 P.G.A. European Tour player Barry Lane shows no signs of tension at address. The hands hang freely, the knees are flexed, and the body is parallel to the target. He is in an excellent position to swing the club.

2 In the first stage of the backswing, the left arm has pushed the club away from the ball, and the clubhead has moved inside the target line as the shoulders begin to turn.

3 Halfway back, Barry's shoulder turn is starting to pull the hips away from the ball, and his wrists have begun to cock.

4 The position at the top of the backswing is perfect. The clubshaft is horizontal to the target line and pointing at the target. The shoulders have turned a full 90 degrees, while the hips have resisted the shoulder turn; the left knee has broken in toward the right, the weight is on the right foot, and Barry's eyes are still focused on the ball.

5

6

7

8

9

[5] Halfway down, Barry's hips are square to the target line and have pulled the club down toward the ball. Notice how the right heel has come off the ground even this early in the swing, a sign that the weight has been transferred onto the left foot.

[6] Just after impact, the hands are continuing to chase the ball. The right heel has come fully off the ground and the eyes are still focused on the original position of the ball.

[7] Just past the halfway stage in the through-swing, the head is just beginning to lift because of the natural turning action of the shoulders. Notice also how the right knee has kicked in toward the target.

[8] The weight has transferred fully to the left leg. The hands are nice and high, with the front of the body facing the target.

[9] A well-balanced finish.

THE SWING PLANE

Many golfers are mystified by the term "swing plane," perhaps because it sounds too much like a geometrical expression. In reality, the swing plane is a very simple concept.

Every golfer has an individual swing plane, one that is determined by the player's physique and the position of the ball in relationship to the stance and setup.

Quite simply, the swing plane runs on an imaginary line, which extends from the ball up through the player's shoulders. The angle of this line is determined by the golfer's stature. For example, a short player, such as Ian Woosnam, will generally have a flatter (nearer horizontal) plane because he will more than likely stand further away from the ball. A tall player, such as Greg Norman, will stand closer to the ball and will therefore have a steeper angle of descent and a more upright (closer to vertical) swing plane.

The swing is most natural when it follows the correct path determined by a player's stature and his relationship to the ball. That's why top players talk about getting into the proper groove. Nick Faldo, for example, is often described as "swinging perfectly up and down the line," because you could draw a straight line from the ball through Nick's shoulders and to his hands at the top of his backswing.

A player who tries to swing flatter or more upright than normal is merely fighting what is natural, increasing his chances of not returning the clubhead to the proper position at impact. Too upright a swing will return the clubhead at too steep an angle of attack, causing a choppy, weak stroke. Too flat a swing inhibits the free movement of the arms, resulting in loss of clubhead speed and, consequently, distance.

It is quite possible to play golf well with a swing that deviates from the correct plane for your body. Many professional players do so. However, as you aren't able to devote endless hours to practice, you will make the game easier for yourself by swinging on the correct plane for your body.

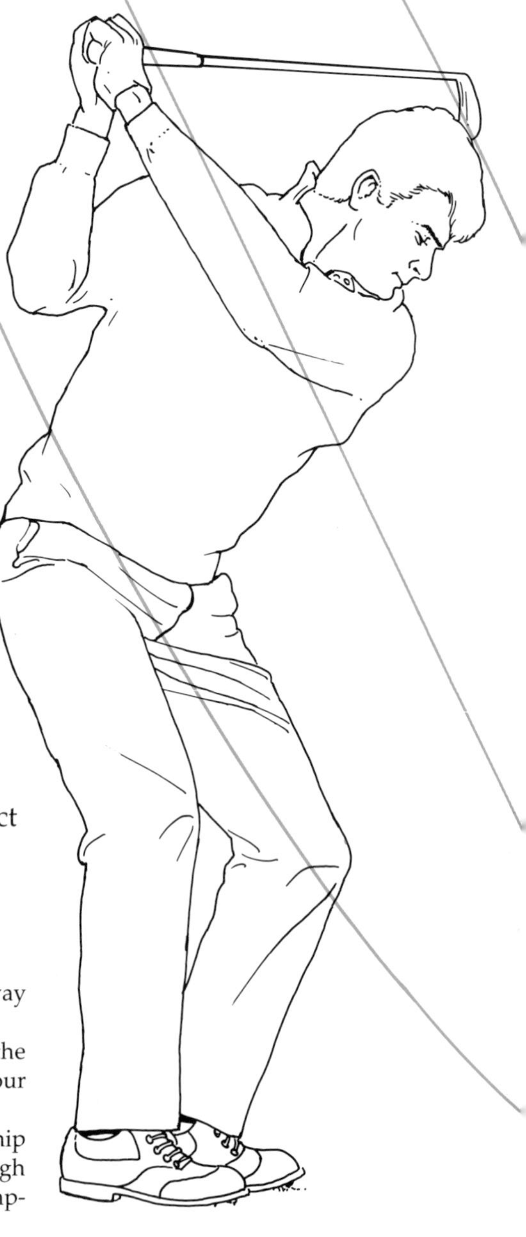

THE SWING PLANE

The swing plane is determined by a player's physique and the distance he stands away from the ball.

The plane of the swing is an imaginary line that runs from the ball up through the shoulders. When you swing, you should do so at this angle. This will ensure that your swing is following the natural arc dictated by your individual stature.

This illustration shows Nick Faldo at the top of his backswing. Notice the relationship between the left arm and the ball. If you were to draw a line from the ball up through Nick's left shoulder, his left arm would extend along that line. There is nothing complicated about this swing; it is totally natural for Nick's physique.

Too flat a swing will inhibit the arms from swinging freely because the body will get in the way. This results in loss of clubhead speed, distance and accuracy.

A swing plane that is too upright allows the arms to swing, but creates too steep an angle of descent. This results in a weak, choppy stroke.

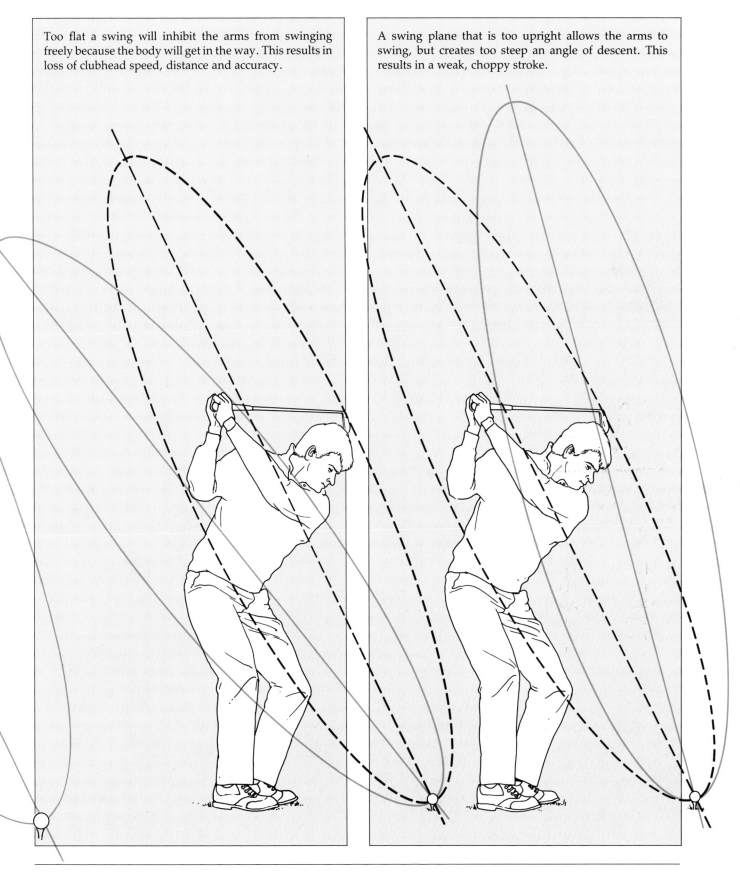

THE DRIVER

The driver is the hardest club to use, because it naturally dictates that you stand further away from the ball. It is also the club which produces the least amount of backspin and the most sidespin. Because backspin counters sidespin, the driver is the one club that golfers tend to have most trouble with. You can slice your drives, even if you hit your short irons straight.

With the driver, you should sweep the club through the ball on a level path, or even slightly on the upswing, at impact. For this reason you tee the ball up higher than any other club.

Position the ball opposite your left heel and tee the ball up so that the top of the driver is even with the center of the ball. Your hands should be in line with the ball at address. This ensures that you get maximum carry and roll from the shot.

The stance for the driver should be the same width as your shoulders. Most players have an overwhelming tendency to try to hit the ball hard with the driver. Ironically, rather than producing power, this action usually results in wayward shots. Distance depends on clubhead speed, which in turn is determined by a longer arc. You should concentrate on achieving a smooth, unhurried swing. When swinging the driver, try to treat it as if it were a seven iron. This will allow you to swing more slowly and evenly, and add yards to your drives.

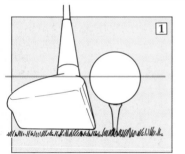

STEP 1
Tee the ball up so that the top of the driver is parallel with the equator of the ball. This ensures that you will hit the ball level, or slightly on the upswing, at impact. Teeing the ball too low encourages a steep angle of approach, which results in a weak, glancing blow.

STEP 2
Position the ball opposite the left heel and set the feet so that the distance between the insteps is the same as the width of your shoulders (A). This is the widest stance that you will adopt, and one that provides a solid base from which to swing.

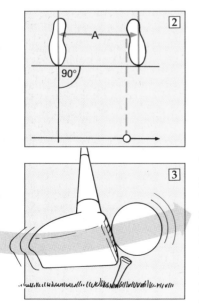

STEP 3
Try to sweep the ball off the tee at impact, instead of hitting down on it as you would with an iron club. A good image to keep in mind is that of swinging through the ball, rather than of hitting at it. Imagine that the ball is part of the arc of the swing and simply gets in the way of the clubhead. This will help you to concentrate on making an unhurried, smooth swing.

TEE SHOT
Tom Watson (U.S.A.) puts everything into this tee shot with his driver. With this club you want to sweep the ball off the tee, rather than hit down on it as you would with an iron. The fact that Watson's tee is still in the turf is proof that he has swept the ball away.
INSET: Greg Norman, one of the longest hitters on the tour.

STAR TIP
To help him hit the ball on the upswing, Greg Norman (Australia) doesn't ground his driver at address. This ensures that he doesn't catch the turf at impact, which would decrease the distance he hits the ball. It is a trick he learned from Jack Nicklaus, and one many average players would do well to copy.

FAIRWAY WOODS AND LONG IRONS

Average golfers find these clubs hard to use, especially the three wood, because the impact position has to be exactly right to guarantee a perfect shot.

Unlike the driver, which is hit slightly on the upswing, and the medium and short irons, which are hit with a descending blow, the fairway woods and long irons must sweep the ball away cleanly off the turf. This means that the sole of the clubhead has to be exactly level with the turf at impact.

Like the driver, the fairway woods and long irons are fairly straight-faced clubs, and do not impart as much backspin as, say, a six or seven iron. Any errors, therefore, will be exaggerated; like the driver, these clubs produce the biggest margin for error.

The stance is slightly narrower than that for the driver, and the ball is moved back toward the center of the stance. In this way you can sweep the ball off the turf, rather than hitting down on it. Push the club away from the ball on a low shallow arc in the backswing to promote the required sweeping action.

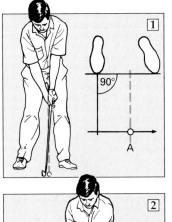

THE LONG IRON
Sandy Lyle cracks a shot away with a long iron. Not too much grass has been uprooted at impact, proof that Lyle has approached the ball on the correct shallow angle.

STEP 1
Position the ball further back toward the middle of the stance (A) than you would if you were hitting a driver. The hands should be slightly ahead of the ball at address. This promotes a sweeping blow, which is essential if you are to pick the ball cleanly off the turf. You should stand slightly closer to the ball with the fairway woods and long irons because they are shorter than the driver.

STEP 2
Start the backswing in one piece by pushing the club away with the left arm and shoulder, and by keeping the clubhead low to the ground. Beware of picking the club up too early in the backswing by breaking the wrists. This will decrease the length of your swing arc and result in a loss of distance.

STEP 3
On the downswing you should try to sweep the ball off the turf (B). There is no need to try to take a divot on this shot; simply concentrate on sweeping the clubhead along the turf at impact. Imagine that you are approaching the ball on a shallow arc, from inside the target line. Too steep an angle of descent on the downswing will force the ball into a high trajectory.

THE MEDIUM IRONS

The medium irons – numbers four, five and six – are perhaps the clubs with which the amateur golfer feels most comfortable. These are the clubs that a professional will give to a beginner, because the shafts are midway between the longest and shortest clubs.

Because the swing plane moves from flat to upright as you move through the bag from driver to wedge, the mid-irons dictate that you will be swinging on the most neutral plane – one that is neither too flat nor too upright.

Unlike the long irons, which are used to hit the ball for distance only, the mid-irons are used to hit the ball a precise distance – the operative word here being precise. For average golfers the five iron is used for a range of 150-160 yards (137-146m), with 10 yards (9m) added on for the four iron, and 10 yards (9m) subtracted for the six.

As they are used on approach shots to the green, there is no need to try to hit these clubs hard; all you need to do is take a five iron instead of a six, for instance, if more distance is required. With the medium irons you should apply backspin to the ball to make it stop quickly when it lands on the green.

STEP 1
The setup for the middle iron requires a square stance, with the ball positioned just left of center (A) in the stance. With the clubhead sitting slightly left of center, the left arm and club shaft should form a straight line to the ball.

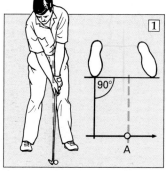

STEP 2
There is no need to rush any swing. The backswing for the middle iron begins with the club being pushed straight back from the ball by the left arm and shoulder, and the weight shifts onto the right leg. The shoulder turn will bring the club back on the inside of the target line and up to the top of the backswing.

STEP 3
Unlike the long iron, which should be swept off the turf, you will hit down into the ball with more of a descending blow with the mid-irons (B) because of the shorter shaft and ball position. The downswing begins with the left hip turning back toward the target, pulling the left arm down into the ball. Then hit through the ball, making sure you contact the ball first and then the turf. This will produce the backspin needed to stop the ball.

PERFECT BALANCE
Payne Stewart (U.S.A.) shows perfect balance after hitting a medium iron. The follow-through is not as long for medium irons as it is for longer clubs. With medium irons you are trying to hit the ball a precise distance, rather than a long way.

THE SHORT IRONS

The short irons — numbers seven, eight and nine — and the pitching wedge are the scoring clubs, the clubs that are used to get the ball close to the hole and to set up birdie opportunities. For an average golfer, the maximum distance with the seven iron is about 140 yards (128m), which decreases by 10 yards (9m) per club as you move down to the wedge.

The swing for the short iron is very upright compared with other clubs, because the short shafts dictate that you must stand nearer the ball.

The most important factor to remember with the short irons is that you never swing flat out. Trying to hit the maximum distance will upset your tempo and timing. Indeed, when you are caught between, say, hitting a full eight iron or a three-quarter seven, hitting the three-quarter shot is always the better choice. This way you won't feel that you have to force the shot, but rather that you can concentrate on making a good, rhythmical swing.

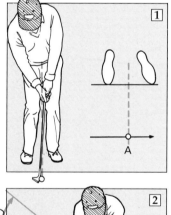

STEP 1
The stance for the short iron, particularly the wedge, is the narrowest you will have to adopt for any full shot, with the feet quite close together. The ball should be back toward the center of your stance (A) and the hands further in front of the ball than on any other full shot.

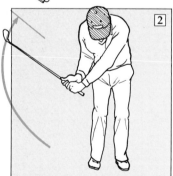

STEP 2
Don't consciously try to cock the wrists early, as this will happen naturally at about hip height. Many amateur players make the mistake of trying to swing the club back to parallel at the top of the backswing. Remember, you do not need to make a full swing on this shot. Once you have swung back just past three-quarters, you should think about beginning the downswing.

STEP 3
With the short irons, the downswing is initiated by the turning of the left hip, which pulls the shoulders and the arms into the swing.

As the arms enter the hitting area, the wrists should remain fully cocked. It is only as the hands near the address position that they uncock and hit down and through the back of the ball. This will make the ball rise on a high trajectory and produce the backspin (B) necessary to make the ball stop quickly on landing.

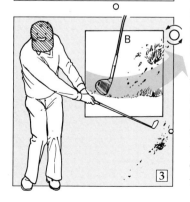

SHORT-IRON APPROACH SHOT
Ronan Rafferty (Northern Ireland) hits a short-iron approach shot. The short irons are the scoring clubs — those used to get the ball close to the hole. The flying turf is a good sign that Rafferty has hit down and through the ball, producing the backspin necessary to stop the ball on the green.

STAR TIP
Seve Ballesteros maintains that a seven iron is the best club to practice with. Although Seve practiced with an old three iron as a youngster, he says that the seven iron promotes an upright swing with its 38 degrees of loft and its short shaft. An upright swing does not deviate too much from the target line throughout the stroke, and the golfer therefore has a better chance of returning the club correctly to the ball at impact.

THE BASIC PITCH SHOT

Ask professionals which aspect of the game is the most important, and almost all will say the short game. You may be able to drive the ball 250 yards (229m) off the tee and hit the irons fairly well, but you will never master this game if you can't play the short shots around the green.

These are the shots which make or break a round, the ones which ultimately determine how well you score.

All golfers face the pitch shot many times during the course of a round. This is especially true of average players, because they do not hit the greens with their second shots most of the time. It is important, then, that average golfers become proficient at this shot.

The pitch shot is not a power shot. It is played anywhere from 90 yards (82m) away from the green, but usually within the 50-yard (46m) range.

PITCH SHOT
Steve Jones (U.S.A.) grips down the handle of his pitching wedge to play this pitch shot. Sliding the hands down the grip gives Jones more control on these feel shots. Jones' club is still entering the turf as the ball rises, proof that he has struck the ball with a descending blow.
INSET: Tom Kite pitching to the green.

 STAR TIP
Tom Kite (U.S.A.) is one of the best players in the world with the pitching wedge. Part of his success stems from his tempo. He only swings the club through to the same height as it was in the backswing. In this way he can simply concentrate on letting the natural loft of the clubface get the ball airborne.

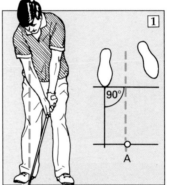

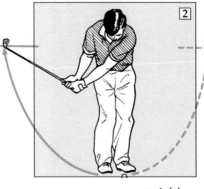

STEP 1
You should take a narrower stance for this shot, with the feet placed about 12in (30cm) apart. Position the ball in the center of the stance (A), so that the hands are ahead of the ball. This shot is best played with an open stance to promote left-to-right spin, which helps the ball land more softly on the green. It is also important to keep your weight on the left foot during this shot. This will promote a crisp strike, and get the ball into the air.

STEP 2
The backswing is quite upright for the pitch shot and is facilitated by the arms and shoulder turn; your hips should remain passive during this shot, unless it is over 50 yards (46m) — but even then they do not play an important role. The wrists are kept firm in the pitch shot, and the natural loft of the club flights the ball high in the air.

STEP 3
The hands should be in front of the clubhead at impact. Many beginners make the mistake of trying to scoop the ball off the turf, which often makes the ball land well short of the green. In this shot it is important to hit the ball first, and then the turf (B). This will send the ball up into the air quickly. In the follow-through, the hands should end up at about the same height that they reached in the backswing.

HIGH AND LOW PITCH SHOTS

THE PITCH-AND-RUN SHOT

[1] An open stance is required for the pitch-and-run shot, with the ball played back in the stance. The arms and hands take the club away from the ball, and the clubhead should never get any higher than hip height.

[2] The hands and arms swing the club back down to the ball on the same line as the takeaway.

[3] The right knee has kicked in slightly toward the target just before impact, and the eyes are fixed on the back of the ball.

[4] Just after impact the left side has cleared out of the way to allow the arms to swing through toward the target. The hands and arms have not quit on the ball, but have continued to swing toward the flag.

[5] This is about as high as the ball will go on this type of shot. The ball will land on the green and roll up toward the hole.

THE LOB SHOT

1 The ball is played well forward in the stance for the lob shot, and the wrists break quite early in the takeaway.

2 The head remains steady for this shot, and the club is swung back with the hands and arms only. This is a feel shot and should be played with a nice, slow backswing.

3 Unlike the normal pitch shot, you should use the natural loft of the wedge to slide the clubface under the ball. Keep the wrists firm and the hands moving slightly ahead of the ball throughout this swing.

4 Just after impact, ensure that the left wrist doesn't collapse. Beware of flicking your wrists; this can cause you to hit the ball flat, or scull it across the green. Notice how in this picture the left wrist has not collapsed.

5 Do not try for a full follow-through on this shot. Only swing the club through to the same distance that you swung it back from the ball.

THE CHIP SHOT

Like the pitch shot, the chip shot is frequently used by all golfers. This is because even the best players in the world do not hit the green every time with their approach shots.

The chip shot can be played with a variety of clubs, from the five iron to the sand wedge. Many average players limit themselves by trying to play every chip with only one club, usually a pitching wedge. This requires an inordinate amount of feel, because they have to learn how to hit the ball different distances in the air. Ultimately what you should aim to do is chip the ball onto the green and let it run up to the hole; the longer you can keep the ball on the putting surface, the better. This requires only one action, which can be used for different clubs.

The key to playing this shot is feel. You must be able to judge how far the ball is going to run on the green with each club. Practice using different clubs from just off the green.

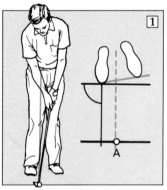

STEP 1
The stance for the chip shot is quite narrow, with the feet very close together. Play the ball back in the center of the stance (A), with the hands ahead of the ball and the weight on the left foot. Point your body left of the target line for this shot, so that there is room for your arms to swing freely through the ball. Grip down the shaft for better feel and control.

STEP 2
There is no wrist action on this shot. Remember, you are only trying to chip the ball onto the green and let it run to the hole. You should take the club straight back from the ball with the arms on as low a line as possible.

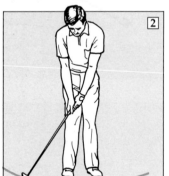

STEP 3
You should only brush the top of the grass with the sole of the clubhead (B) on the chip shot. It is vital to keep your head still throughout this shot; it is the one shot which allows you to actually see the ball being hit. If you see the clubhead striking the ball, you have kept your head steady. Keep your left wrist firm throughout this shot. By pulling through the shot with the left wrist and arm, you will ensure that the hands don't merely flick at the ball through impact. Try to imagine that you are playing the chip with your hands in a cast. This will help eliminate any wrist action.

CHIP SHOT OVER A BUNKER
Seve Ballesteros plays a tricky chip shot over a bunker to a flag cut close to the edge of the green. Although the ball is already on its way, Seve's head is in the same position as it was at address.

STAR TIP
Chi Chi Rodriguez has played most of his career with a chipping stroke, which keeps the ball very close to the ground. His philosophy is that it is easier to control a ball that runs most of the way to the hole than one that flies a long way through the air. Watch professional players. They get the ball onto the putting surface as quickly as possible.

CHIPPING TACTICS

LET THE BALL RUN TO THE HOLE

You should keep the ball on the putting surface for as long as possible (see page 38), but to do this you must learn to use a number of clubs. Start with the six iron, and try chipping to the same spot on the green with each club.

It is important that you play the same type of stroke with each club. That way all you have to learn is one action, rather than trying to manufacture shots for different situations. Once you have learned the basic technique, it is only a matter of judging the length of the back-swing.

Make a mental note of how far the ball rolls after it lands. This will help greatly when you have to play the actual shot in a round of golf.

1 Try chipping with a variety of clubs to get a feel for the amount of run each club produces. The less lofted the club, the more run on the ball. This is by far the safer shot, as it gets the ball onto the putting surface quickly.

A six iron B seven iron C eight iron D nine iron E pitching wedge F sand wedge

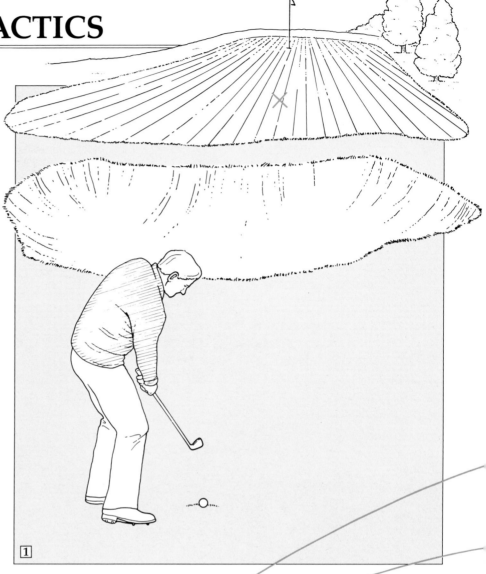

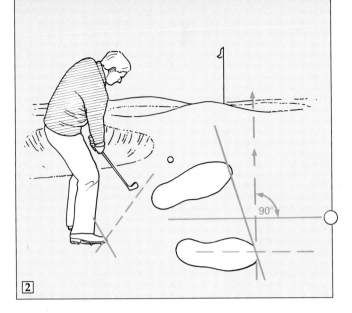

2

TAKE AN OPEN STANCE

Use an open stance on chip shots (in which the feet point left of the target). Because the swing is mainly with the arms, the open stance will get the body out of the way and let the arms move unhindered. Remember that your feet should be very close together for this shot, as this will also force you to swing the arms.

2 Adopt an open stance so that your body does not get in the way of your arms.

HIT DOWN TO POP THE BALL OUT OF THE ROUGH

To play a pitch shot out of heavy rough, play the ball back in the stance; place the hands ahead, break the wrists early on the backswing, and focus on hitting down into the back of the ball. Open the clubface slightly, as the long grass will tend to wrap around the hosel and close the clubface. It is important that you keep the weight on the left foot throughout this shot, to ensure that you strike the ball with a descending blow. Striking down into the back of the ball will pop it up into the air and onto the green.

3 Place the ball back in the stance, and the hands ahead. Place the weight on the left foot and hit down to pop the ball out of the rough.

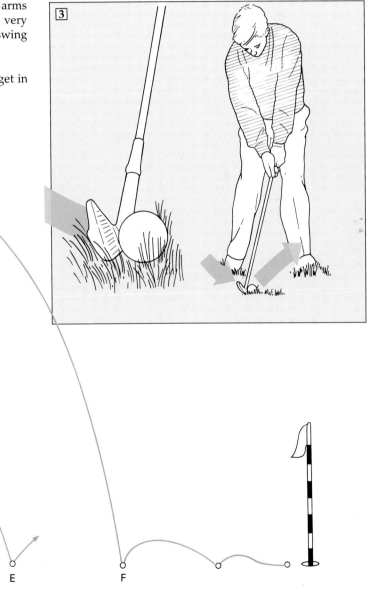

3

C   D   E   F

THE PUTTING STROKE

Every once in a while, you will hear professionals refer to the "other" game of golf, to the "game within the game." They are talking about the game played on the green – putting – that part of golf where it all counts.

Although you may have a technically sound game from tee to green, it all counts for nothing unless you can get the ball in the hole. After all, nearly half the strokes you take in a round of golf will be on the green. The famous expression "It's not how, but how many" never applied more than to the putting stroke.

Most professionals seem to have developed their own individual method of putting. For them, technique and style are not as important as getting the ball into the hole.

Although there are many ways in which you can execute the putting stroke, there are some basic techniques which learners should adhere to in order to guarantee a sound stroke. Your own individual stroke will develop from these techniques in time. Try to develop a stroke that is simple and repeats under pressure.

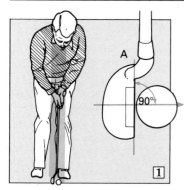

STEP 1

Ensure that your hands are parallel to the putter face and that your eyes are directly over the ball at address. This guarantees that you will return the blade square to the line (A), and that you will be able to see the line all the way to the hole.

STEP 2

Like the chip shot, there is no wrist break in the putt. When stroking the putter, you should do so with the arms and shoulders moving like a pendulum. The triangle formed by the hands, arms and shoulders (B) should remain constant throughout the stroke.

STEP 3

It is vital to keep your head steady when stroking the putt. The action is with the arms and shoulders; any lower body action will ruin the shot. All good putters accelerate the putter through the ball at impact, and you should try to copy this action. One of the best ways to ensure that you accelerate the putter at impact is by keeping the left wrist firm (C) throughout the stroke. Try not to hit past the left wrist, but against it when making the stroke. The wrist should also never bend or stop moving on the forward stroke, or you will decelerate through the ball.

PUTTER
Ben Crenshaw (U.S.A.) is perhaps the best putter in the modern game. The secret of his success lies in his technique. Crenshaw's hands, arms and shoulders work as one unit throughout the putting stroke, ensuring that the smaller muscles in the hands play as little part in the stroke as possible.
INSET: Jack Nicklaus judges the line of a putt.

STAR TIP

Throughout his career, Jack Nicklaus has played with a putting stroke in which he adopts a crouched stance, hunched right over the ball. Nicklaus has adopted this position because it is the only one which allows him to get his eyes directly over the ball at address. This way, he is better able to see the line that the putt will be travelling down.

THE GAME WITHIN THE GAME

[1] Plumb bobbing – Curtis Strange uses his putter to check the direction the grass is growing on the putting surface.

[2] Scotland's Sam Torrance deviates from the norm by using a long putter. Torrance switched to this putter to overcome the "yips." He found that he couldn't control the nerves in his hands with a normal putter. The long putter is guided by the right hand only, therefore eliminating the use of the smaller muscles in the hands and wrists.

[3] The reverse-overlap grip is the one most favored by professionals because it allows all the fingers of the right hand to be placed on the grip. Placing the left forefinger straight down over the top of the fingers of the right hand also stops the left wrist from breaking during the stroke.

[4] Nick Faldo successfully strokes a putt toward the hole. Faldo's wrists have remained firm throughout the stroke. This is a must if you are to accelerate through the ball.

[5] Bernhard Langer (Germany) employs a grip in which he clamps the butt of the putter up against his left wrist. This grip works for Langer because, being a left-handed player, he makes the putt entirely with the left hand and wrist. Langer adopted this grip to overcome the "yips."

6 No other part of the game is as frustrating as the one played on the green. Here Ian Woosnam shows his frustration after missing a birdie putt.

7 Although there are some fundamentals that must be adhered to to guarantee success on the green, putting is the one part of the game that can be very individualistic. Japan's Isao Aoki uses a putting stroke in which the hands are very low and the putter head is pointing almost straight up in the air. Unorthodox maybe, but very successful.

8 Putters come in all shapes and sizes depending on individual taste. D. A. Weibring (U.S.A.) uses one with three plastic balls to help him line up better. He simply places the putter head behind the ball so that all four balls are in line.

9 Lining up the ball is important. After marking the ball on the green, Payne Stewart replaces it so that the manufacturer's logo is pointing at the hole. This helps him line up the putter's blade.

10 Two pairs of eyes are better than one. Tom Kite and Curtis Strange survey a putt in the 1989 Ryder Cup matches.

11 Jack Nicklaus shields his eyes from the sun to make it easier for him to determine the slope of the green.

THE BASIC BUNKER SHOT

Theoretically, the bunker (or sand) shot should be the easiest to play in golf, because it is the only one which doesn't actually call on you to strike the ball. Ironically, it is for this very reason that it is one of the toughest shots to play.

Average players also find this shot hard because it is not permitted to ground the club at address (to do so will incur a two-stroke penalty).

The sand shot can be played successfully, provided that you understand the basic techniques involved and have the confidence to carry them out.

For this shot, you should enter the sand behind the ball with the sand wedge. How far you enter the sand behind the ball will depend on the distance you are from the flag. Generally speaking, the further you are from the hole, the closer to the ball the club enters the sand.

The basic shot requires you to hit the sand about 2in (5cm) behind the ball. With the sand wedge's heavy flange, the club will skid or splash underneath the ball, lifting the ball out on a cushion of sand.

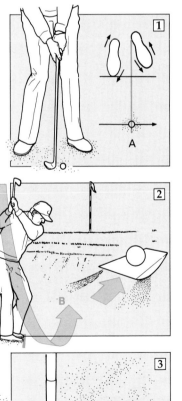

BASIC TECHNIQUE
The basic technique on sand shots calls for the club to enter the sand about two inches (5cm) behind the ball, lifting the ball out on a cushion of sand. England's Howard Clark demonstrates this technique successfully in this picture.

STEP 1
Set up to this shot with the ball opposite your left heel (A) and with your body pointing to the left of the flag. The blade of the club should be opened fractionally for a normal bunker shot, and much wider for a higher shot. Twist your feet into the sand at address to guarantee a good foothold, and to help you get under the ball at impact. Twisting your feet into the sand also helps you determine its consistency.

STEP 2
On the backswing, you should swing along the line of your shoulders with only your hands and arms. Because you have addressed the ball with an open stance, the swing path will be to the left of the target (B). This produces a shot which slices through the sand, ensuring that the ball comes out softly.

STEP 3
Don't let the left wrist break on the downswing, as this will cause you to flick at the ball. Keep the left wrist firm as the clubhead goes through the sand, and the ball will fly softly onto the green. Don't slow the arms after impact. Keep them swinging through to a high finish.

BUNKER TACTICS

4 Howard Clark plays a long bunker shot. This shot is one of the most difficult in golf. It calls for the clubhead to enter the sand about an inch (2.5cm) before the ball, rather than the normal two inches (5cm). To play this shot, set up so that you are not as open as for a regular bunker shot. Ensure that the clubface is square and to the target.

5 Balance is the most important factor when the ball is below your feet. Dig in with your right foot to ensure a good foothold, and bend your left knee as much as possible to lower your body to the ball. Aim a little to the left on this shot, as the ball will tend to fly to the right with the slope.

1 You don't always have to use a sand wedge in the bunker. If the lie is good, you can even use a putter, as England's Roger Chapman has done in this instance.

2 The technique required to play seaside bunker shots differs from that used to play bunkers on inland courses. A much more upright swing with an early wrist break is required for the type of pot bunkers one finds on seaside courses. In this picture, Japan's "Joe" Ozaki finds himself in the deep pot bunker which fronts St. Andrew's 17th green.

3 Sandy Lyle plays one of the most famous fairway bunker shots of all time. This seven-iron approach shot to the 18th green in the 1988 Masters earned Lyle a birdie putt and the Green Jacket. To play this shot successfully, hit the ball first, and then the sand. Try to nip the ball off the top of the sand, taking as little sand as possible.

[8] It is important not to fight the lie of the sand when the ball sits on an up-slope. Balance is also important, so ensure that your weight is a little forward to stop you from toppling over. Aim about a half an inch (1cm) behind the ball with your weight on your right side, and then swing along the contour of the slope. The ball will fly high, so take this into account when you play the stroke.

🏌 STAR
   TIP

Paul Azinger (U.S.A.) is one of the best bunker players in the world. His success lies in his ability to spin the ball out of the sand. Although a tall man, Azinger sits down on these shots, lowering his body so that he can more easily slide the club under the ball. He also practices his bunker play diligently — a tip most golfers would do well to follow. Practicing regularly will take any fear out of the shot.

[6] One of the best shots to play when the ball is at the back of the bunker up against the lip is a low running shot. Position the hands well ahead, with the ball back in the stance beside the right foot. Keep the weight on the left foot, then pick the club up sharply and hit down on the ball. It will run through the bunker and onto the green.

[7] Play the ball in the middle of your stance when it sits above your feet. Aim right, as the ball will fly to the left; grip down the handle of the club, put most of your weight on your toes, and then play a normal bunker shot. Try to minimize body movement, as this will throw you off balance.

SHAPING THE BALL

The ability to work the ball, to move it from left to right (a fade), from right to left (a draw), or to hit it high or low, is important when you are out on the course. You need to be able to use these tactics when you are confronted by obstacles on the course, or when the wind is strong.

There is no mystique involved in shaping the flight of the ball. With a little practice, the average player can learn how to get himself out of trouble without having to make drastic changes to the basic swing.

THE FADE
To play the fade, simply take the stance you would take if you were playing a normal shot, but aim your body to the left of the target. Keep the clubface aimed at the target. Then simply swing along the shoulder line. The ball will start to the left of the target and drift back to the right.

THE DRAW
This shot is exactly the opposite of the fade — it starts right and curves to the left. To play this shot, simply aim the clubface at the target and take your normal stance, pointing your body to the right of the target. Again, it is simply a matter of swinging along the shoulder line.

LOW SHOTS
To play the low shot, play the ball back in the stance, keep the hands ahead of the ball, grip down the club, and keep your weight on the left foot.

Putting the weight on the left foot and the hands ahead restricts the backswing. The ball should be hit with a punching action, keeping the follow-through as short as possible.

THE HIGH SHOT
Set up to play the high shot by placing the ball well forward in the stance, and keep the clubface open. On this shot you should keep the hands level with the ball at address, and the weight on the right side throughout the swing. Concentrate on making a long, high follow-through.

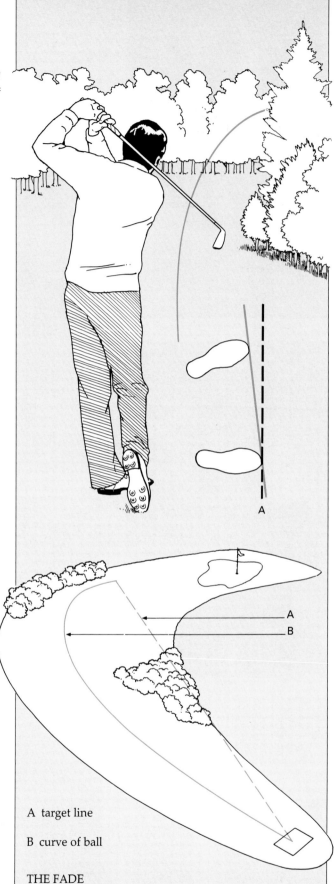

A target line

B curve of ball

THE FADE
To fade the ball, set up with an open stance, so that the body is aimed left of the target, keeping the clubface square to the target. Then simply swing the club naturally. The ball will start left, and then move to the right.

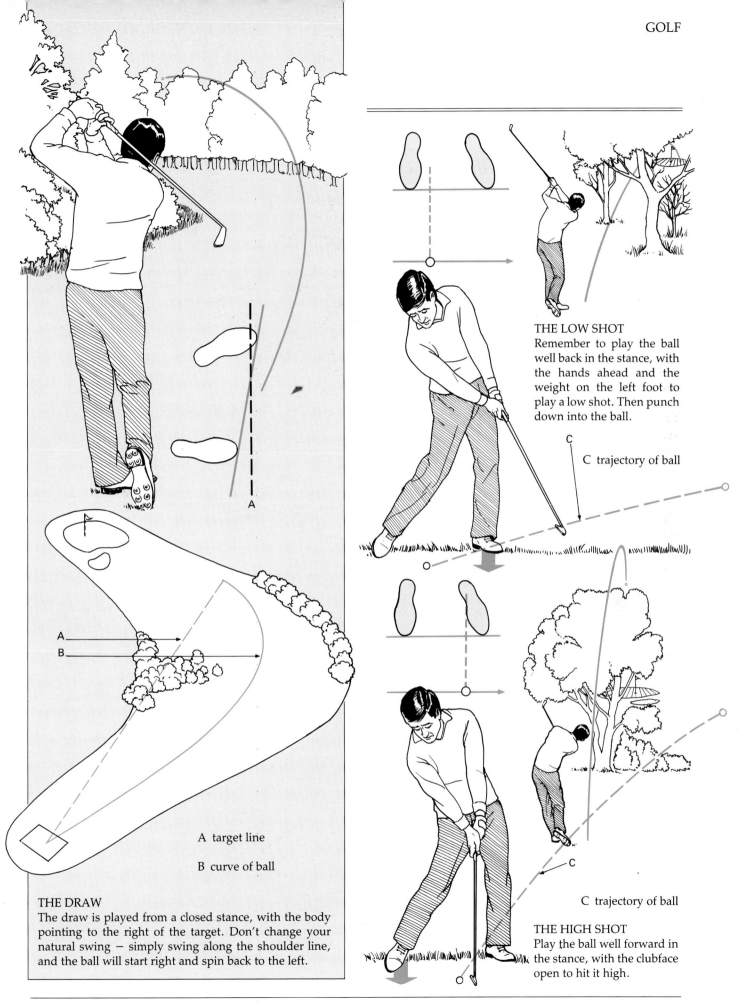

THE LOW SHOT
Remember to play the ball well back in the stance, with the hands ahead and the weight on the left foot to play a low shot. Then punch down into the ball.

C trajectory of ball

A target line

B curve of ball

THE DRAW
The draw is played from a closed stance, with the body pointing to the right of the target. Don't change your natural swing — simply swing along the shoulder line, and the ball will start right and spin back to the left.

C trajectory of ball

THE HIGH SHOT
Play the ball well forward in the stance, with the clubface open to hit it high.

SLOPING LIES

UPHILL LIE

As with all shots played from an awkward lie, the main problem uphill is maintaining your balance. Try to tilt your body to the right so that you are working with the slope, not against it. Make sure that your right foot is perpendicular to the target line at address. This will stop your body from swaying to the right in the backswing.

The ball tends to fly quite high on this shot because of the uphill slope, so take more club (for example, a five iron as opposed to a six) than normal. It will usually move from right to left, and you must allow for this.

1 Place your weight on your right foot when playing from an uphill lie. This will help you tilt your body with the slope and enable you to swing along the slope of the ground. Take more club than normal, as the ball will fly quite high.

DOWNHILL

The ball will run further when you have a downhill lie, so take less club than you would need normally (for example, a seven iron rather than a six). Again, you don't want to fight the slope, so set your body at a right angle to it. Pick the club up, and then hit down the slope. You should chase the club after the ball, so make sure you hit down and through the ball. Allow for the ball to fly to the right.

2 Play the ball back in the stance when playing from a downhill lie. This will encourage you to swing along the slope and to hit down on it at impact. Tilt the body to the left so that it is perpendicular to the slope. The ball will run a long way on this shot, so take less club to compensate.

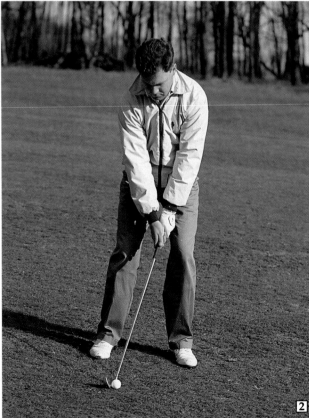

BALL ABOVE FEET

A ball which sits above the feet promotes a flatter swing than normal. Set up by standing more erect, put the weight forward to guard against falling back during the backswing, and move the hands further down the grip of the club for better control.

This shot will tend to fall with the slope, so aim to the right of the target at address.

3 Stand a little more erect and place the weight forward when the ball is above your feet. You will tend to swing flatter than normal because of the slope, and the ball will move from right to left. Compensate by aiming further right than normal.

BALL BELOW FEET

The ball will move from left to right with the slope, so aim left at address.

Set up with the weight back on the heels to stop you from falling over; grip the club at the top of the handle, widen your stance, and try to swing only with the hands and arms. Aim to the left, as the shot will bend in the same direction as the slope.

4 The ball will move from left to right when it is below your feet, so allow for this by aiming left. Grip as far up the handle as possible to counteract the slope, and take a three-quarter-length backswing, using only the hands and arms.

SHOTS FROM THE ROUGH

No golfer can produce a swing that will hit the ball straight every single time. As a result, playing from rough grass is a problem common to all players.

The best philosophy any player can adopt is to be realistic. Always play the shot that is going to, at the very least, get you back into play. Don't try to play an ambitious shot if the ball is lying knee-deep in grass. If this means having to settle for bogey, remember that it is better to swallow your pride and lose only one stroke instead of several.

With every shot you play in a round of golf, you put backspin on the ball. This is what makes it fly in a certain trajectory. However, backspin can only be applied when the clubface cleanly strikes the ball. The more grass there is between the clubface and the ball, the less backspin will be applied. As a result, the ball will fly lower and run further, so take this into account when playing the shot.

STEP 1

If you are playing a shot from heavy rough, set up with the ball back in the stance, the hands ahead and the clubface open. Remember to open the clubface, as the long grass tends to wrap around the hosel at impact, closing the face. Set your weight on the left foot, as this will promote a descending blow. This is vital if you want to get the ball out.

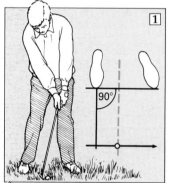

STEP 2

Pick the club up steeply on the backswing by breaking the wrist early to promote a

steep arc. Don't take a full swing on this shot; at most take a three-quarter-length backswing. This will provide more control.

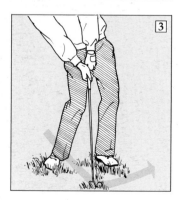

STEP 3

On the downswing, hit down steeply behind the ball to pop it out of the grass. Lead the downswing with the hands and keep your grip firm so that the grass doesn't twist the clubhead. Punch down into the grass with a firm, descending blow. It is important that you hit down behind the ball, so keep your eyes on a spot where you are trying to hit the grass. You won't get much of a follow-through on this shot because you are punching down into the grass.

DEEP ROUGH
Greg Norman plays out of deep, heavy rough during the Open Championship. INSET: heavy rough didn't stop Seve Ballesteros from winning the 1988 Open Championship at Royal Lytham. Here he chases after a shot during the first round.

GOLF'S GEOMETRY

Many golfers play badly because they have never sat down and actually thought about the real purpose of the golf swing. If they have, they have forgotten what it was long ago. To play golf well, you need to return the clubface squarely to the ball on the correct line. That is all you need to do.

There are only three directions in which the clubface can be pointing at impact: open, closed, or square.

The same is basically true for the swing path. It, too, has only three directions from which the clubhead can approach the ball: outside the target line (a), inside the target line (b), and straight along the target line (c).

The above factors, along with the angle of approach and the speed of the clubhead, influence the behavior of the ball and produce the common faults outlined below.

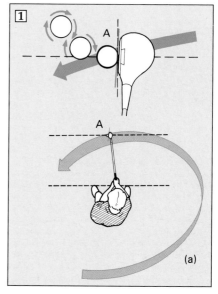

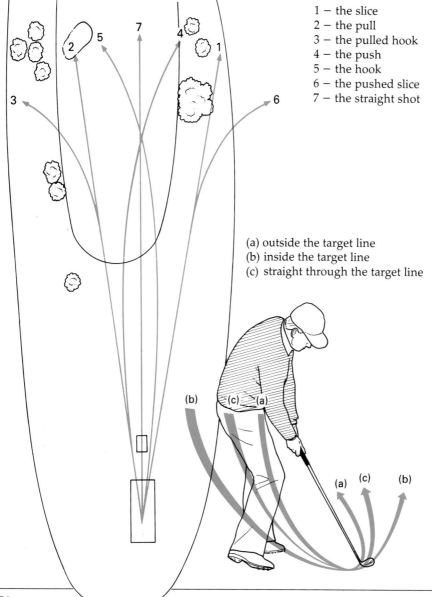

1 – the slice
2 – the pull
3 – the pulled hook
4 – the push
5 – the hook
6 – the pushed slice
7 – the straight shot

(a) outside the target line
(b) inside the target line
(c) straight through the target line

THE SLICE

The ball starts left and then bends right. This is the bane of most golfers. It is caused by a swing path that approaches from outside the target line to inside with an open clubface (A). The slice is a glancing blow which imparts left-to-right sidespin.

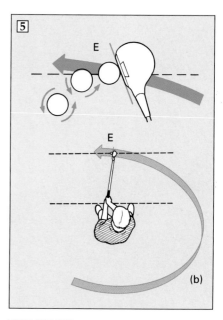

THE HOOK

The ball starts right of the target, and then bends left. Like the push, the clubhead has approached from the inside, but with a closed clubface (E). This combination of factors produces right-to-left side spin.

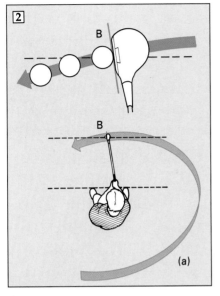

THE PULL
The ball flies straight, but to the left of the target. Again, the swing path is from outside to inside the target line at impact, but this time the clubface is square to the swing path (B).

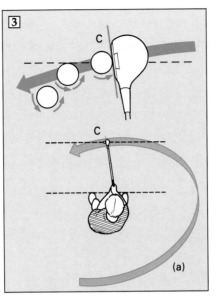

THE PULLED HOOK
The ball starts left of the target and curves further left. This shot is also caused by an out-to-in swing path, but in this case the clubface is closed to the swing path (C) at impact.

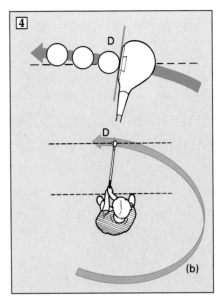

THE PUSH
The ball flies straight, but to the right of the target. This time the clubhead is approaching on an in-to-out swing path; the clubface is square to the swing path (D) causing the ball to fly straight right.

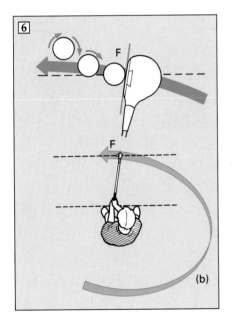

THE PUSHED SLICE
The ball starts to the right, and bends further right. The clubhead has approached from the inside with the clubface open (F), causing a weak, glancing blow. This produces one of the ugliest shots in golf.

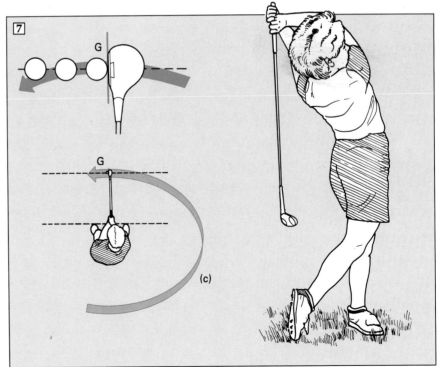

THE STRAIGHT SHOT
The ball starts straight, and continues to fly straight. At impact, the clubface is square (G) and the swing path matches the target line.

ACTION STUDY

In the final round of the 1988 British Open Championship at Royal Lytham and St Anne's, Seve Ballesteros came to the last green with a one-stroke lead over Zimbabwe's Nick Price. Ballesteros' approach shot ended up just to the left of the green, leaving a difficult chip shot to the flag.

This type of shot poses no problems for the professionals under normal circumstances. But in a major championship, even the best players in the world can collapse under pressure. This shot was particularly tricky because it was sitting on a downslope.

With Price on the green with his approach shot, albeit a long way from the hole, Ballesteros knew he had to get the ball close to give himself a chance of winning his fifth major.

Seve not only got it close, he almost holed it, and when Price three putted, Ballesteros had won his third British Open.

The techniques needed to execute this shot are fairly simple. Here's how Seve played the shot.

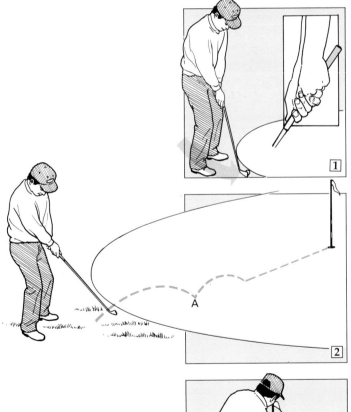

STEP 1

Seve set up for this shot with an open stance, and his weight on his left foot. He bent his knees a little more than normal and gripped down the handle of the club to compensate for the downslope. He decided to play a sand wedge to loft the ball over the small hollow between him and the green.

STEP 2

Seve wanted to get the ball on the surface of the green as quickly as possible and let it run to the flag. This is a strategy which all amateurs should bear in mind before playing the chip shot. Too many golfers try to lob the ball to the hole, and end short or long because they find it difficult to judge how hard they have to hit the ball. Seve chose a spot on the green (A) on which to land the ball and from which he knew it would run up close to the hole.

WILL IT OR WON'T IT? Seve Ballesteros watches his shot to the flag at the 18th hole at Royal Lytham, at the end of the final round of the 1988 British Open Championship.

STEP 3

With his weight left and his hands ahead of the ball, Seve kept his wrists firm and hit down into the back of the ball with a descending blow, to pop the ball up into the air over the hollow and onto the green. He kept his arms swinging through toward the target after he had struck the ball. The ball lipped the cup and finished 6in (15cm) away from the flag.

STRATEGY AND PSYCHOLOGY

When it comes to the thinking side of golf, no one comes close to Jack Nicklaus. No other professional prepares for a tournament in the way he does. Nicklaus never hits a shot until he is ready, and he never attempts to play a stroke that he can't play.

Nicklaus knows exactly what he is going to do from the moment he arrives on the tee. He plays the hole in his mind even before he tees the ball up, taking into consideration the wind conditions, scanning the fairway for trouble, and working out just where he wants the ball to land for his approach shot to the green.

There are many things that make Nicklaus a champion, but in his acceptance of his own limitations he is an example to every golfer. So many golfers attempt the impossible, going for the flag, for instance, when the sensible option would be to play for the fat part (or heart) of the green.

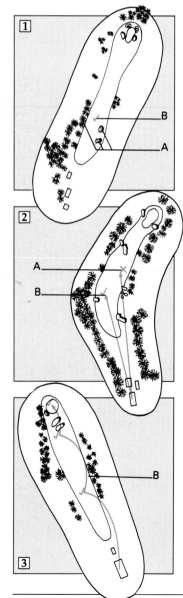

STEP 1

From the moment you arrive on the tee, you should be scanning the fairway for danger areas (A), and picking an area in which you want the ball to land (B) so that your approach shot to the green will be relatively easy. Check the wind conditions, too — they will determine how you should play from the tee.

A danger   B safe

STEP 2

Your number one priority off the tee should be to put the ball in play in the best possible position. For example, on a dogleg par four, you should weigh up all the options before you decide to try to cut the corner (A). It may be that on this particular shot, you should forget about trying to cut the distance on the hole, and settle for playing a longer iron into the green. This may also be true if there is water to carry off the tee. Sometimes it may be better to play short of the water (B), and hit a longer iron into the green.

A danger   B safe

STEP 3

You should be as cautious from the fairway as you were off the tee. Study the trouble around the green, and then decide on the type of shot you wish to play. Sometimes it is better to play safe (B) than gamble and be buried in the face of a bunker.   **B safe**

STRATEGY
Jack Nicklaus selects a club from long-time caddie Jimmy Dickenson. Nicklaus is the consummate player, never playing a shot until he has weighed up all the options.
INSET: Ben Crenshaw and his caddie assessing distance.

STAR TIP
In the final round of the 1984 Masters Tournament, Ben Crenshaw arrived at both the par fives on the inward nine, with a decision to make on the 13th and 15th holes. He had to judge whether or not to lay up short of the green, or to attempt a long carry over the water. After weighing up all the possibilities, Crenshaw decided to lay up on both holes, and went on to win the Masters by two strokes.

ETIQUETTE

Every golfer who opens the rule book is immediately confronted with a small section on etiquette. This section should be read before a golf club is even picked up for the first time.

The section on etiquette does not lay down rules *per se*, so much as a code of behavior to follow on the course. This code of conduct is simple and based on nothing more than courtesy and common sense; it points out ways in which you can play the game without disturbing others, and emphasizes the important principle of leaving the course in the exact condition in which you found it.

The points covered by the etiquette section are listed below:

SAFETY
- When taking a practice swing or playing a stroke, you should ensure that no one is standing nearby or in a position where they may be hit by the club, the ball or any stones or twigs during the stroke.

CONSIDERATION FOR OTHER PLAYERS
- A player making a stroke is entitled to common courtesy. Other players should not interrupt by talking, moving or standing nearby while the stroke is being played.
- Players should play without delay, but not until the group ahead has moved out of range.
- When searching for a lost ball, the players in the group behind should be allowed to play through.
- Players should leave the green immediately after the hole has been played.
- All divots should be replaced.
- Bunkers should be raked smooth after the stroke has been played.

[1] Payne Stewart repairs a pitch mark made by his approach shot to the green. It is entirely within the rules to do this, and will be appreciated by other players on the course.

[2] Ian Woosnam marks his ball with a small coin. It is common courtesy to mark your ball when it is on the putting surface, as it can serve as a distraction to your playing partners.

[3] Quiet, please! Marshals at the U.S. Open hold up signs telling the gallery to keep quiet while José Maria Olazabal plays his tee shot. Remaining silent while the golfer is teeing off is one of the first rules of etiquette. It is also important to stay well out of the way when a player is executing a stroke.

[4] After playing his bunker shot, Irishman Des Smyth has his caddie rake the sand smooth. All players should rake the bunkers after they have finished their stroke. This will ensure that anyone playing a similar shot afterwards will have an even lie.

RULES AND HANDICAPS

KNOW THE RULES

Perhaps the most important thing you can put in your bag after your clubs is a copy of the rule book.

For a small investment, this compact little book will pay huge dividends in the future. With this in your bag, you can settle disputes and queries on the spot.

It pays to have a good knowledge of the rules; it can mean the difference between ruining a hole and escaping with just a bogey. For example, when it comes to water hazards, there are different options available depending on the type of hazard. You will be penalized for putting your shot into the water, but that is the time to consider all the choices open to you. For instance, there is nothing to be gained from dropping a ball within two club-lengths of the hazards if the grass is long and wet. Better to drop in a good lie behind the water hazard, making sure you keep the point of entry between the hole and the spot on which the ball is dropped.

Tom Watson is a player who, over the years, has gained an excellent understanding of the rules, and has used them to his advantage.

HANDICAPS

Golf is a unique sport, in that players of different abilities can compete against one another in a match. Jack Nicklaus, for example, could compete against a player who may never shoot below 90. The handicapping system allows such a match to take place.

Basically, the handicapping system measures a player's average performance, and is calculated over a number of rounds. In Great Britain, for example, a handicap is calculated after a player has played three rounds over the same course. The handicap committee then decides on a handicap that is based on the number of strokes by which the average score differs from the Standard Scratch Score (the score which a player with a handicap of zero is expected to return on a given course).

THE SCORECARD

A player is required to make sure that the handicap entered on the scorecard is correct. If the handicap on the card is higher than his actual handicap, a player will be disqualified from competitions. If it is lower than his actual handicap the score will stand.

A player will get strokes on certain holes, depending on the handicap. The index on the card determines the holes on which strokes are given. For example, an eight-handicap player will get strokes on holes marked from one to eight, while a sixteen-handicap player will get strokes on holes marked from one to sixteen.

A player is only required to count the gross number of strokes taken on each hole for scoring. He will then subtract one or more strokes if his handicap allows him a stroke on the hole.

UNPLAYABLE

If a ball is unplayable (A), the rules of golf allow you to drop the ball as far back as you want, provided you keep the point where the ball lay between the flag and the spot you intend to drop the ball (B). There is a one-stroke penalty.

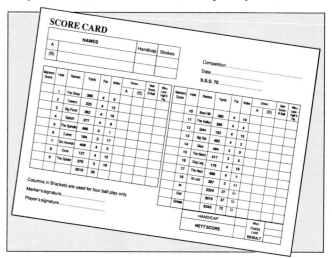

HANDICAP SYSTEM

The handicap system allows players of differing abilities to play against one another by allotting strokes to the higher handicap player on certain holes.

MOVABLE OBSTRUCTION
If a movable obstruction impedes your swing, you are allowed under the rules of golf to move the obstruction.

AGAINST THE FLAGSTICK
A ball played from off the green which rests against the flagstick (A) is deemed to be in the hole if it drops into the cup when the flagstick is removed.

CORRECT PROCEDURES
It is important that all players know the correct procedures when it comes to dropping the ball (two club lengths).

WATER HAZARD
There are five options open to the player whose ball enters a lateral water hazard. Knowledge of these options can save you from further setbacks.

PRACTICE WITH A PURPOSE

Many golfers make the same mistake when they go to the practice ground — that is, if they go to the practice ground: many don't — they practice those aspects of their game at which they are already proficient. As a result, the areas they need to work on continue to be neglected.

This is a natural tendency, but one that doesn't do anything to improve your play.

The practice ground should be the place you go to to work on those parts of your game that plague you when you play. An honest appraisal after every round should be made, so that when you get to the practice ground you know exactly what it is you have to work on. This appraisal will give you an objective, a target to aim at, whether it is as simple as developing a sound chipping stroke or learning to draw the ball.

Above all, you should pay close attention to the basics of the swing — grip, stance, posture, alignment and your overall setup to the ball. It is a good idea to place a club pointing in the direction of the target, and then to practice hitting shots with your feet parallel to the club. This will ensure that you are standing square to the target line.

Jack Nicklaus has a good philosophy when it comes to practicing. He never hits any shot, in practice or otherwise, to which he hasn't given all his concentration and effort.

Whether he is alone on the practice fairway or in the heat of a major championship, Nicklaus approaches every shot the same. Many golfers simply go to the range, beat a bucket of balls, usually with the driver, and feel they have practiced, when all they've really done is wasted energy and ingrained into their swings the very faults they sought to eradicate in the first place.

1

2

1 José Maria Olazabal practices under the watchful eye of long-time coach Jesus Arrutti. Having someone who knows your game to watch you swing can solve your problem in minutes.

2 The successful partnership of David Leadbetter and Nick Faldo has enabled Faldo to become one of the best golfers in the world.

3 The professionals spend long hours on the practice range working on fundamentals. Even a tenth of that time spent working on basics is well worth while if you are an amateur.

4 There is no substitute for professional instruction. Taking lessons from a qualified teacher will cut strokes off your game.

5 Bob Torrance (center) tees up a ball for Ian Woosnam. Torrance has become one of the most respected coaches in Europe as a result of his work with top European professionals.

Like Nicklaus, you should give your practice shots the utmost attention. Use your practice to develop a pre-shot routine, one that allows you to aim the clubhead and the body correctly every time. Watch, too, how the ball reacts when you hit shots. The flight of the ball reveals everything about your swing. By analyzing the trajectory of the ball, you can pinpoint faults in your game.

Trying to do too much is another mistake that amateurs make on the practice ground. You will never learn everything in one practice session. It is better to work on one fault, correct it, and then move on to another. In some cases, it may take only a few shots to analyze a problem and put it right; in others, it may take up your whole session. Never move on to something else until you have rectified the first fault.

Keep your practice sessions interesting by using your imagination. Don't simply beat balls. Aim at different targets and try different clubs. Try playing an imaginary round on the range, so that you play the clubs you might play around your own course. In this instance, though, you get to play them until you hit them perfectly.

TESTING YOURSELF

One of the quickest ways to improve is to appraise your game honestly. This will not only determine what you should practice, but will also help you when you play.

As stated in the previous section, you should analyze each round you play. Go over the score card after every round and count the number of fairways hit off the tee, the number of greens hit in regulation, the number of times you got up and down in two shots out of a bunker or from off the green, and the number of putts you used.

If, for example, you took only 31 putts but shot 102, then your problem is obviously not on the greens, and you should look at other parts of your game. If you hit only one or two fairways during the round, you should work at becoming more proficient with the driver.

As was also mentioned in the last section, playing games is one way to keep practice sessions interesting. Another way is to mark yourself during your practice session. For example, take 10 balls and try to chip them into an umbrella. In the practice bunker, hit 10 balls from the sand and give yourself a mark out of 10 based on the number of balls that end up within, say, 3ft (1m) of the pin; you can do the same with chip and pitch shots. On the practice green, try placing 10 balls in a 5ft (1.5m) circle around the cup and see how many you hole. On long putts, see how many of the 10 balls end up within a 3ft (1m) circle of the hole.

For the long game, you could designate an imaginary fairway about 30 yards (27m) wide, and see how many out of 10 drives end up landing in that area. On iron shots, pick a marker and see how many shots out of 10 land in what would be putting distance.

Such exercises will help you to improve because you will always be striving to better your best score. The dividends on the course will be obvious.

1 CHIPPING
Simple exercises such as chipping balls into an umbrella will sharpen your short game immensely. Try to better the number you get into the umbrella each time.

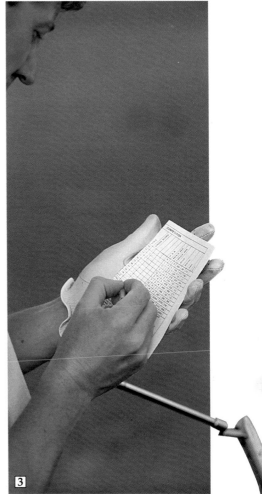

2 CIRCLE DRILL

The circle drill is one of the best exercises for short putts. First place balls in a 3ft (1m) circumference around the hole, and then try to sink every one before moving on to a 5ft (1.5m) circle.

3 APPRAISAL

Give your game an honest appraisal after every round. Count the number of fairways and greens hit in regulation, the number of putts, the number of times you got the ball up and down from a bunker, etc. This will tell you which parts of your game need to be improved.

GLOSSARY

Address – the position taken by the player when setting up to play a stroke.

Albatross – three strokes below par on a hole.

Alignment – position of the body in relation to the target.

Approach shot – a shot played to the green.

Arc - the swing path of the clubhead.

Backspin – reverse spin which causes the ball to stop quickly when it lands.

Backswing – movement of the club away from the ball to the top of the swing.

Birdie – one stroke below par on a hole.

Blade – name given to a shot which is hit with the leading edge of the clubhead, causing it to run along the ground. Also the name given to traditional forged clubs and types of putter.

Block – term given to a shot in which the hands don't turn over naturally at impact, causing the ball to fly to the right.

Bogey – one stroke over par on a hole.

Break – the amount a ball will deviate from a straight line on the putting green.

Bunker – depression in the ground, usually filled with sand.

Caddie – someone employed to carry a player's clubs and give advice on playing the course.

Chip – short, low running shot played from off the green.

Closed clubface – when the clubface is pointing to the left of the target.

Closed stance – to address the ball with the body pointing to the right of the target.

Clubface – front of the clubhead which actually makes contact with the ball.

Clubhead – part of the club which strikes the ball.

Cut shot – a shot which flies high and moves from left to right.

Divot – piece of turf taken out of the ground when striking the ball.

Dogleg – a fairway that runs straight and then bends to the left or the right before it reaches the green.

Dormie – a player is dormie when he is as many holes ahead of an opponent as there are left to play; for example, four up with four to play.

Downswing – movement of the club from the top of the backswing to the ball.

Draw – a shot that moves from right to left.

Drive – a shot hit from the tee, usually on a par four or five.

Driver – number one wood; the club with the least loft, capable of hitting the ball the furthest.

Duck hook – a low shot which starts left of the target and curves further left.

Eagle – two strokes below par on a hole.

Equipment – anything used by the player or caddie when playing, including clothes, clubs, golf balls and trolleys.

Explosion – shot played from the sand.

Fade – shot which starts straight and curves slightly to the right.

Fairway – the mown area of the course between the tee and the green.

Fat shot – a shot in which the clubhead enters the ground before hitting the ball.

Feathery – an early type of ball, made from feathers stuffed into a leather casing.

Flagstick – movable pole with an attached flag which indicates the position of the hole.

Flange – that part of the sole of the clubhead which protrudes at the back.

Flat swing – a swing which moves on a close to horizontal arc around the body.

Follow-through – the final part of the swing which occurs after impact.

Fore – a warning shouted to players ahead to warn them of an approaching ball.

Forward press – slight forward movement of the hands prior to the beginning of the backswing.

Fourball – match in which two players play their better ball against the better ball of their opponents.

Foursome – match in which two partners play alternate shots using the same ball.

Grain – the direction the grass is growing on the green.

Green – the putting surface or the closely mown area around the hole.

Grip – the position of the hands on the club. Also the handle of the club.

Guttie – forerunner of the modern ball, which was made of *gutta percha*.

Handicap – the number of strokes a player receives to bring his score down to par. For example, someone with a 14 handicap who has shot a gross score of 86 has actually shot a net 72.

Hazard – any bunker or water hazard.

Heavy shot – similar to a fat shot, where the club digs too far into the ground, reducing power and decreasing distance.

Heel – the part of the sole of the clubhead closest to the shaft.

Hole − a 4¼ in (11cm) diameter hole cut in the putting surface.

Honor − the privilege of hitting first off the tee.

Hooding the clubface − tilting the clubface toward the target at address to hit a low shot.

Hook − shot that bends from right to left.

Hosel − the area of the clubhead where it joins the shaft.

Insert − piece of material inset into the face of a wooden club.

Iron − metal-headed club.

Lie − the angle between the sole of the clubhead and the shaft. Alternatively, the manner in which the ball is lying on the grass.

Line − the preferred direction of the shot.

Links − a seaside course.

Loft − the angle formed by the clubface and the ground when the club is soled correctly at address.

Major − a term applied to the four biggest championships in golf: the Masters, the British Open, the United States Open and the United States Professional Golfers' Association (USPGA) Championship.

Offset − the distance between the leading edge of the clubface and the front portion of the hosel.

Par − the normal amount of strokes required to play a hole. Par is generally set according to length. A par three is never longer than 250 yards (229m); a par four is for holes between 251 and 475 yards (229 − 434m); and a par five is for 476 yards (435m) and longer.

Pin − another term for the flagstick.

Pin high − shot which ends level with the flagstick, but not necessarily straight.

Pitch − short, high shot to the green.

Pitch and run − short shot played with a less lofted club which runs a long way along the ground.

Pivot − rotation of the body on the backswing.

Plane − imaginary line which extends from the ball up through a player's shoulder, and the arc on which the club should be swung.

Plugged lie − ball which stays in its own pitch mark.

Pull − shot which flies on a straight line to the left of the target.

Punch − shot which flies low to the ground.

Push − shot which flies straight, but to the right of the target.

Putt − shot played with a putter on the green.

Putter − straight-faced club

used on the green.

Release − the act of uncocking the wrists at impact.

Rough − long grass.

Run − the distance the ball travels along the ground.

Sand wedge − heavy, soled club used to play out of bunkers.

Scratch − term given to someone with a handicap of zero.

Shank − shot in which the ball is struck with the neck of the club.

Short game − those shots played around the green.

Skull − shot in which the ball is struck with the sole of the club.

Sky − shot, usually played with a wooden club, which flies straight up into the air.

Slice − shot which bends drastically from left to right.

Sole − the bottom of the clubhead.

Square stance − when the body is parallel to the target line.

Stance − the placing of the feet when addressing the ball.

Stroke − the act of making contact with the ball.

Stroke play − form of golf where a player counts the number of strokes taken to play a round.

Swing − the entire action taken when hitting the ball.

Takeaway − the beginning of the backswing.

Tee − peg used to raise the ball above the surface of the teeing ground.

Teeing ground − the area from which the first shot is played on a hole.

Texas wedge − expression given to a shot played from off the green with a putter.

Thin − shot on which the sole of the club does not make contact with the entire ball but only part of it, producing a low, running shot.

Top shot − shot which catches only the top half of the ball.

Trap − another expression given to a bunker.

Turn − the rotation of the body during the backswing.

Upright swing − swing which travels on an arc close to vertical.

Waggle − movement of the clubhead prior to the swing.

Wedge − lofted club designed for pitch shots.

Wood − wooden-headed club.

Yips − a nervous condition causing twitching in the hands and wrists. It plagues golfers particularly on putting greens.

INDEX